All colle
   are so:

A 2 - 10
B 11 - 19
C 20 - 43
D 44 - 50
E 51 - 54
F 55 - 62
G 63 - 69
H 70 - 73
I 74 - 77
J
K 78
L 79 - 84
M 85 - 92

N 93 - 94
O 95
P 96 - 109
Q
R 110 - 121
S 122 - 139
T 140 - 152
U
V 153
W 154 - 160
X
Y 161
Z

A Flight of Airplanes

A

Collection

of

Antiques

An

Orchard

of

Apple Trees

A Bushel of Apples

A Stack of Arms

A Sheaf of Arrows

A

Museum

of

Art

A Trove of Artifacts

An

Album

of

Autographs

A

Bunch

of

Bananas

A String of Beads

A

Convoy

of

Bicycles

… 14

A Shower of Blows

A

Library

of

Books

A Loaf of Bread

A

Pile

of

Bricks

A

Hail

of

Bullets

A

Hedge

of

Bushes

A

Deck

of

Cards

A

Line

of

Cars

A

Block

of

Cheese

A

Row

of

Chairs

A

Set

of

China

A

Packet

of

Cigarettes

A

Box

of

Cigars

A

Bank

of

Circuits

A

Mound

of

Clay

A Closet of Clothes

A

Sky

of

Clouds

A

Set

of

Clubs

A Cluster of Coconuts

A

Collection

of

Coins

A

Palette

of

Colors

An Unease of Compromises

A

Network

of

Computers

A Shower of Confetti

A Batch of Cookies

A Crop of Corn

A

Bale

of

Cotton

An

Alliance

of

Countries

A Cabinet of Curiosities

A

Wad

of

Currency

A

Cache

of

Data

A

Cluster

of

Diamonds

A

Pile

of

Dirt

An

Array

of

Dishes

An

Binder

of

Documents

A

Chest

of

Drawers

A

Cloud

of

Dust

A

Pair

or

Earrings

A Clutch of Eggs

A Chain of Events

A

Book

of

Exercises

A

Fold

of

Fabric

A Roll of Film

A Series of Films

A Cord of Firewood

A

Block

of

Flats

A Bouquet of Flowers

A

Basket

of

Fruit

A Suite of Furniture

A Compendium of Games

A Set of Gloves

A Catalogue of Goods

A Sheaf of Grain

A Bunch of Grapes

A Meadow of Grass

A Battery of Guns

A Lock of Hair

A

Bale

of

Hay

A

Range

of

Hills

A

Row

of

Houses

(74)

A

Block

of

Ice

A Wealth of Information

A Sketchbook of Ideas

An Archipelago of Islands

A Bunch of Keys

A

Pile

of

Laundry

A Packet of Letters

A

Pack

of

Lies

A

Spectrum

of

Light

A Litter of Litterboxes

A

Fleet

of

Lorries

A

Stack

of

Magazines

An Atlas of Maps

A

Course

of

Meals

A

Cache

of

Memories

A Shower of Meteors

A

Bank

of

Monitors

A

Range

of

Mountains

A

Display

of

Merchandise

A List of Names

A

Book

of

Notes

A

Slew

of

Options

A Palette of Paints

A

Stack

of

Pancakes

A

Ream

of

Paper

A

Tray

of

Pastries

A
Tapestry
of
Patterns

A

Necklace

of

Pearls

A Pack of Pencils

A Collection of Pens

An Album of Photographs

A Set of Phrases

A Gallery of Pictures

A

Solar System

of

Planets

An Anthology of Poems

A List of Prices

A Bundle of Rags

A Shower of Rain

A

Archive

of

Records

A

Collection

of

Relics

A Rabble of Remedies

A Library of Resources

A Bowl of Rice

A Network of Roads

A Suite of Rooms

A

Heap

of

Rubbish

A

Heap

of

Ruins

A Nest of Rumors

A

Heap

of

Sand

A

Pair

of

Scissors

A

Fleet

of

Ships

An

Armada

of

Ships

A Pair of Shoes

A Column of Smoke

A

Fall

of

Snow

A Drawer of Socks

A Carton of Soda

A

Array

of

Solar Panels

A

Batch

of

Software

A Bed of Soil

A Flight of Stairs

An Album of Stamps

A

Galaxy

of

Stars

A

Union

of

States

A

Flight

of

Steps

A Bundle of Sticks

A Nest of Tables

An

Agenda

of

Tasks

A Fleet of Taxis

A Library of Texts

A

Spool

of

Thread

A Stand of Timber

A Twinkling of Todays

A Promise of Tomorrows

A Set of Tools

A Fleet of Trains

A

Trove

of

Treasures

A

Forest

of

Trees

A

Wall

of

Trophies

A

Collection

of

Vinyl Records

A Sheaf of Wheat

A Farm of Windmills

A

Cellar

of

Wine

A

Bundle

of

Wires

A Tuft of Wood

A

Bale

of

Wool

A Vocabulary of Words

A Multitude of Yesterdays

Made in the USA
Las Vegas, NV
09 April 2025